Journalistic Techniques to Boost Your Content Marketing

Copyright © 2023 Reginaldo Osnildo
All rights reserved.

PRESENTATION

INTRODUCTION

THE IMPORTANCE OF JOURNALISM IN CONTENT MARKETING

NARRATIVE AND STORYTELLING

INTERVIEWS AND RELIABLE SOURCES

INVESTIGATION AND RESEARCH

DATA COLLECTION AND STATISTICS

CONTENT EDITING AND REVIEW

CHOOSING RELEVANT TOPICS AND ANGLES

ENGAGING THE AUDIENCE WITH CAPTIVING TITLES

THE INFLUENCE OF SOCIAL MEDIA ON CONTENT JOURNALISM

SEO AND KEYWORDS: THE PERFECT MARRIAGE

MEASURING THE IMPACT AND SUCCESS OF CONTENT

LONG-TERM CONTENT PLANNING

CONTENT DISTRIBUTION STRATEGIES

FINAL CONSIDERATIONS

READING SUGGESTION

REGINALDO OSNILDO

PRESENTATION

You're about to dive into a complete guide on how to apply journalism techniques to content marketing [1]. Over the next few chapters, you will learn everything from basic concepts to advanced strategies that will transform the way you produce and distribute content.

Each chapter has been carefully crafted to provide valuable insights and practical actions that can be implemented immediately. You'll walk away from this book with an in-depth understanding of how to tell engaging stories, conduct captivating interviews, mine data, optimize for SEO, [2]and much more.

But this book is not just theoretical. It was made for content producers like you. Therefore, all concepts are explained in a simple and direct way, with examples and case studies that demonstrate how to apply these techniques in the real world, or rather, phygital [3].

By the end of this book, you will be able to take your content to a new level. Your audience will be more engaged, you will attract more leads [4]and all of this will translate into concrete results for your business.

So without further ado, dive into this definitive guide to journalism for content marketing. The next chapters will bring insights that can transform your content strategy. Good reading.

Reginaldo Osnildo

Note: "Some of the real-life examples presented in this book are in Portuguese."

INTRODUCTION

If you're reading this book, you probably already have some idea of the importance of content marketing. But even if you are an experienced content producer, it is always worth remembering the basic concepts and why this strategy is so powerful.

This chapter will recap what content marketing is, its main objectives and benefits. You will see how content has become a strategic asset for companies and professionals who want to stand out.

In addition, success stories, data and statistics that prove the ROI [5] of content marketing will be presented. You will come away from this chapter with complete clarity about why you should invest time and resources in this strategy.

WHAT IS CONTENT MARKETING?

Let's start by defining exactly what content marketing is. In a nutshell, it is the creation and distribution of relevant and valuable materials to attract and convert a target audience.

The focus is on producing content that really helps the public, providing useful information and insights that solve pain and problems. Unlike traditional advertising, the content is non-intrusive and aims to nurture leads throughout the funnel.

The formats are varied: blog articles, e-books, guides, case studies, videos, podcasts, social media posts, infographics and much more. But what matters is not the form, but the quality and relevance of the content.

Instead of repeating sales and promotions, content marketing seeks to gain the trust and preference of the target audience, positioning your company or brand as an authority in the niche.

MAIN OBJECTIVES AND BENEFITS

Now that you know what content marketing is, what are its main objectives and benefits? To answer this, I made a list:

- **Attract qualified leads** - By offering relevant content for free, you attract people genuinely interested in your business.

- **Increase traffic and links** - Quality content improves SEO and generates links and mentions from other sites.

- **Generate insights about the target audience** - By constantly producing content, you better understand your leads.

- **Increase sales** - Content nurtures leads throughout the funnel, increasing conversions.

- **Build customer loyalty** - Content creates relationships with the audience and generates returns.

- **Position your brand** - Your content shows your expertise, gaining authority in the niche.

- **Reduce acquisition costs** - Leads generated by content cost less than paid ads.

As you can see, there are several benefits to content marketing. The next sections will bring real cases and data that support these results.

SUCESS HISTORIES

One of the best ways to understand the effectiveness of content marketing is by looking at examples of companies that have had significant results with this strategy.

Moz [6], a reference in SEO, saw its traffic and leads increase after investing in high-quality content, such as extensive blog posts, e-books and free webinars. Moz has taken a unique approach to content marketing, focusing on authenticity, leveraging user-generated content, investing in SEO, and providing value to its target audience. Moz's experience offers several important lessons for companies looking to build a successful content marketing strategy, such as being authentic, leveraging user-generated content, investing in SEO, and providing value to your target audience. Even on the day I revisited the Moz website, while I was writing this material for you, they updated a super guide [7].

Por: Vitória Umurhurhu
6 de novembro de 2023

O guia definitivo para planejamento de conteúdo [modelo gratuito]

Marketing de Conteúdo | Indústria de Marketing

As opiniões do autor são inteiramente próprias (excluindo o evento improvável da hipnose) e podem nem sempre refletir as opiniões de Moz.

Este artigo foi publicado originalmente em 4 de setembro de 2012 e atualizado e atualizado em 6 de novembro de 2023.

PR agency Shift Communications gained more leads by focusing on content rather than press releases. A really cool case that is on the company's blog is a campaign to promote two new Big Mac sizes, using paid media, organically earned media and own leads. The campaign included a vending machine that dispensed free, fresh Big Macs. The campaign aimed to attract new millennial [8] consumers and engage consumers who had moved away from the Big Mac. The campaign also wanted to create attention and media coverage for the vending machine event. This generated a lot of buzz [9] on social media and in the press, using the hashtags [10] #BigMacForThat and #BigMacATM. The campaign also received [11] positive feedback from consumers who tried the new products and praised the taste and quality of the Big Macs [12].

Contently, a content management platform, presents numerous cases with content production that reflect the company's success [13]:

- Scotiabank built a financial education hub and increased organic search traffic.

- Dell Perspectives grew its audience by 200% through bold social impact storytelling.

- UPMC generated 144 thousand user actions and became one of the most reliable sources in the healthcare area.

- The American Kennel Club increased traffic by 30% and thrived with a small team.

- Bank of the West is rewriting Finserv 's content playbook with sustainability narratives.

- Cardinal Health's content distribution strategy increased traffic by 3x.

- ENI brought its industry expertise to life through video.

- Walmart's content program increased shopping cart size by 7%.

- Marriott doubled its monthly traffic to more than 500 thousand consumers.

These are just a few examples of companies that prove the power of content marketing when done consistently and strategically.

But content marketing isn't just about business cases. Many professionals and influencers have grown exponentially by creating valuable content on social media.

One example is entrepreneur Marie Forleo. With her YouTube channel, she generates thousands of views teaching digital marketing and personal life [14].

Another success story is Neil Patel. As a blogger and inbound marketing consultant, he has become a respected authority in the online world [15].

These examples show that content creators of all sizes and niches can achieve great results with this strategy.

WHY CONTENT MARKETING WORKS?

But after all, why does content marketing work so well? What are the reasons that explain the high ROI of this strategy? These are not questions that can be answered so easily, as if there were a magic formula (although I am saying that there is a content marketing formula, it is not magic). What we do know is that some circumstances drive content marketing success. Some of the main reasons are:

- **Content attracts qualified leads**, with real interest in your business - different from leads generated by ads that click without purchasing intention.

- **It positions** your company or personal brand as an authority in the niche, which generates credibility and preference.

- Unlike traditional advertising, **the content is not**

intrusive. It adds value to the public.

- Over the long term, content **generates engagement and nurtures leads** through the funnel, increasing sales.

- It also significantly improves **organic discovery**, with SEO and links from other sites.

- And **the more content you produce, the more you learn** about your target audience and their interests.

Content marketing works because it builds relationships, trust and authority. It positions your brand subtly, without being invasive. Therefore, it generates consistent returns over the long term.

NUMBERS AND STATISTICS

Numbers are also crucial to prove the importance of this strategy. So, see some statistics about content marketing in 2023:[16]

- 82% of marketers actively invest in content marketing

- 40% of B2B marketers have a content marketing strategy to attract customers

- 69% of marketers actively invest in SEO to attract leads

- 67% of marketers say content marketing effectively generates leads

- 51% of companies that invest in content marketing publish content every day

- 81% of marketers see content as an essential business strategy

Content is here to stay and is one of the pillars of digital marketing today. These data speak for themselves. They prove that content marketing is chosen as a significant strategy for any business.

In the next chapter, you will see in more depth the relationship between content marketing and journalism. We'll look at how you can draw inspiration from traditional journalism to create powerful, engaging content.

I hope you have a good understanding of what content marketing is and the significant results that this strategy can bring to any brand or business. Content is the best way to attract qualified leads and build relationships nowadays.

Start planning your content schedule now and put into practice the tips you will learn in the next chapters. With consistency and strategy, you will see your leads and sales grow gradually. Content marketing really works, you just need to know how to apply it correctly.

THE IMPORTANCE OF JOURNALISM IN CONTENT MARKETING

In the previous chapter, you saw an introduction to what content marketing is and why this strategy is so powerful. Now it's time to dive deeper into a crucial area for creating content that truly engages and converts: journalism.

In this chapter, we will analyze why journalism is essential for content marketing today. You will see how to apply renowned journalism techniques to make your content more engaging, informative and strategic.

Are you curious? So let's start.

THE EVOLUTION OF CONTENT MARKETING

Before talking about the relationship with journalism, it is important to understand how content marketing has evolved over the years.

In the beginning, many companies saw content as just a way to generate links and improve SEO. The focus was on volume and quantity, not necessarily quality.

Over time, the content became more strategic. Brands started to invest in more elaborate formats such as e-books, infographics, videos and podcasts.

However, in many cases, the content was still superficial, focused on selling rather than really adding value. Download and view rates were high, but engagement was low.

Nowadays, there is a much greater demand for quality content. With so much information available online, producing superficial or tedious material no longer achieves results.

That's where journalism comes in. Applying journalistic techniques to content marketing has become crucial to create materials that truly connect with the audience and generate engagement.

WHAT JOURNALISM CAN TEACH

Journalism emerged with the aim of informing people about relevant and current facts in an ethical and empowering way.

Although content marketing has commercial objectives, it can draw inspiration from much of what makes journalism so engaging and effective when it comes to conveying information.

Some of the main elements of journalism that can be applied to marketing content:

- **Fact finding** - Checking data and sources to ensure the accuracy of what is being said.

- **Objectivity** - Present information impartially, without bias or sensationalism.

- **Contextualization** - Provide backgrounds and explanations for the public to understand the subject clearly.

- **Humanization** - Show the human side behind the facts, with stories and testimonials.

- **Research** - Dig deeper into topics, bringing angles and insights that the public is unaware of.

- **Multimediality** - Combining texts, images, audio and videos to enrich the narrative.

- **Relevance** - Cover what really interests the reader, not just what is convenient for the source.

Little by little you will realize how these journalistic elements can make your content much richer and more engaging.

THE POWER OF NARRATIVE IN CONTENT MARKETING

One of the biggest lessons that content marketing can absorb from journalism is the power of storytelling. Telling a captivating story makes all the difference when creating engaging content. In content marketing, you also want to (or at least should) tell compelling stories and narratives through your texts, videos, and podcasts.

Instead of just throwing out a bunch of loose information, build plots with a beginning, middle, and end. Have an introductory hook, develop the content fluidly and end with a memorable conclusion.

Also include human elements in these narratives. Stories about people and their experiences create an emotional connection with the audience.

Another tip is to be visual. Describe scenarios, situations and details that help the reader transport themselves into the reality you are portraying.

These are just a few examples of how to apply narrative techniques to capture the audience's attention from start to finish in any content format.

CREDIBILITY FOR JOURNALISM IN CONTENT MARKETING

And speaking of capturing the public's attention, another great lesson from journalism for content marketing is credibility.

Journalism is recognized for seeking the truth of the facts before publishing anything. This is achieved through extensive investigation, checking of sources and accuracy of the data presented.

This stance is essential in content marketing too. Do not publish anything that you cannot prove with sources and evidence. **Don't exaggerate or distort data to prove your point** .

This credibility is gained little by little and is what will make the public trust you as a source of valuable information.

Some strategies are:

- Link to your sources, allowing the reader to evaluate the original information.

- Mention studies, experts and recognized bodies in the sector.

- Clearly signal when something is your personal opinion and not an indisputable fact.

- Reveal numbers, rates and any statistics used in the content.

By following these journalistic practices, your content becomes much more trustworthy. And readers who trust what you publish are more likely to become leads and customers in the future.

CONTENT THAT GENERATES RESULTS

So far, you've seen several journalistic techniques that can be used to produce much more engaging content and convert leads.

But we cannot forget that, at the end of the day, content marketing exists to generate results for your business. All content you create must have a strategic purpose behind it.

Therefore, some marketing content practices that differ from pure journalism are:

- Focus on topics aligned with your funnel, that attract your *buyer personas* [17]. Journalism, on the other hand, needs to cover a wider range of topics.

- Segment and target specific content to different target audiences, rather than trying to please everyone.

- Include *calls I'm action* [18] according to the stage of the funnel, inviting leads to take the next action.

- Make sponsored posts and advertisements that expand the reach of your content.

Although storytelling [19] and journalistic techniques are essential, never forget your business objectives. Content needs to generate conversions from a certain point onwards.

Balance quality information with calls to action when the lead is ready to move through the funnel. Contextualize, educating your leads, and then direct them to the next step.

This balance between education and promotion is what makes content marketing so effective.

JOURNALISM IS THE BASIS FOR POWERFUL CONTENT

We reach the end of this chapter with a comprehensive overview of the crucial relationship between journalism and content marketing today.

You saw how journalism can teach essential techniques for investigation, narrative, credibility and contextualization of information.

By applying these lessons to your content, you gain your audience's trust and engage them with interesting and relevant stories and facts.

But also remember the objectives of content marketing, which go beyond informing. Content serves to nurture leads, position your brand and eventually generate sales.

In the next chapter, we will dive into a specific and powerful journalistic technique: storytelling. You'll see practical storytelling strategies in content that hold attention from start to finish.

I hope you understand the value of journalism to create content that actually interests and engages your target audience. Journalistic techniques give credibility and engagement to your marketing content. Little by little you will master them all.

Take advantage of these tips and start applying them now to transform the quality of the content you produce. Remember: valuable information generates trust, and trust generates sales.

NARRATIVE AND STORYTELLING

In the previous chapter, you saw the importance of applying journalistic techniques in content marketing, including the power of narrative to capture the audience's attention.

Now it's time to explore this topic in greater depth. In this chapter, you will see strategies and practical tips for telling captivating stories through storytelling in your content.

Shall we dive into this universe?

WHAT IS STORYTELLING?

First of all, let's define what storytelling is. In a nutshell, it's the art of telling stories in an engaging way to connect with people on an emotional level.

Different from simply presenting facts or data, storytelling creates a narrative around these elements. It puts you inside the story and makes you experience the characters' journey.

Storytelling is used from ancient oral traditions to modern narratives such as cinema, literature and even journalism. And it's a technique that you can carry over to your content too.

Why does storytelling work?

But why does storytelling captivate people so much? What are the reasons that make storytelling so powerful?

Some of the main ones are:

- **Emotional connection:** people identify with characters and situations similar to theirs;

- **Easy to remember:** stories are recorded in our memory more effectively than loose facts;

- **Holds attention:** curiosity to know the end of the story makes the audience continue consuming the content;

- **Creates relationships:** by sharing personal stories, you get closer to the public;

- **Entertainment:** storytelling informs and educates in a pleasant, not boring way.

These are some of the psychological drivers that explain the power of narratives in content marketing and advertising.

Stories inspire, teach and influence people, in a subtle and organic way. Therefore, mastering storytelling will make all the difference in the quality and conversion of your content.

But how to apply storytelling in practice? The next sections provide tips and practical examples.

CHOOSING RELEVANT STORIES

Before you start inventing random stories, you need to understand that not every narrative fits your content. The story needs to be aligned with the theme and bring some value to your target audience.

Some potential sources of stories for your content:

- Success stories of customers who subscribed to your product/service

- Personal stories about you or the origins of your company/brand

- Market research, interviews and insights into the segment

- Data and projections that show historical evolution

- Reports from experts and opinion leaders

- Examples of similar companies that illustrate a concept

- Hypothetical but realistic stories about your ideal customer

Focus on stories that show a transformation - the starting point, the challenges, and how you or your product helps resolve those obstacles.

Choose non-obvious angles that bring a new perspective to the reader. The best stories are the ones he can't find anywhere else.

STRUCTURING THE NARRATIVE

Once you've chosen a good story, you need to structure it in a captivating way. Remember the classic elements of any narrative:

- **Introductory hook** - start by introducing the characters and the initial setting in an intriguing way.

- **Development** - explore the characters' challenges, obstacles, trials and errors to resolve the situation.

- **Climax** - the critical moment in the story, whether a twist, solution or great insight.

- **Conclusion** - close showing the resolution and what was learned at the end of this journey.

Furthermore, bet on non-linear narratives, which use flashbacks, flashforwards and other resources to break the linearity of the story.

Also explore all emotions: joy, sadness, fear, anger, surprise. Make the reader put themselves in the shoes of those characters.

And pay attention to the descriptions and details. The more sensorial and alive, the easier it is for the audience to visualize that scene in their imagination.

VISUAL AND SOUND STORYTELLING

So far we have given examples of storytelling in written content, but narratives can also be told visually and soundly in videos and podcasts.

In these formats, elements such as soundtrack, images and intonation help establish the mood and reinforce the emotions of the story.

In videos, you also have visual resources such as flashbacks, supporting images, infographics and reconstructions, among others.

In audio, voice intonation, soundtracks and special effects help to enrich the narrative. Interviews with the characters in the story also add more veracity.

Regardless of the format, storytelling allows you to develop rich and engaging narratives that connect with the public much more than just facts and loose data.

CUSTOMER STORIES AND SUCCESS STORIES

A very powerful type of storytelling in content marketing is the success story of your company's real customers.

Instead of just listing the benefits of your product/service, tell the story of a customer who solved a specific problem by adopting your solution.

Describe the initial pain scenario, the failed attempts with other alternatives, how he met you and the results after hiring your product/service.

Focus on real challenges and positive transformation. Show concrete numbers and data whenever possible to prove the change.

This practical application and identification with the character make this type of storytelling extremely powerful in helping leads visualize the value of your product in practice.

STORIES ABOUT THE ORIGIN OF YOUR BRAND

Another very common type is storytelling about the origins of your company, product or personal brand.

Tell us in an engaging way what your motivations were, the challenges in the beginning and how your solution was validated in the market.

This is a great resource to humanize your brand and connect with your audience on a more personal level, building relationships.

Explore your learnings, mistakes and twists along the way. Convey your values and purpose behind the brand through this narrative.

This type of story helps your audience identify with you and better understand what your company or brand stands for. This generates empathy and preference.

AFTER-SALES STORYTELLING

Stories can also be powerful post-sales, to engage customers who have already purchased your product/service.

In this case, tell stories about the various ways your product can be used, new use cases, evolutions and improvements over time.

Create content that helps them make the most of available resources, conveying your expertise indirectly through these narratives.

This type of storytelling reduces churn [20] and helps sell expansions and upgrades to current customers. The stories reinforce the value of what they have previously acquired.

THE SKY IS THE LIMIT

There is an infinite number of creative possibilities for applying storytelling in content marketing and gaining leads organically.

Keep the tips in this section in mind and explore different angles, formats and moments to tell relevant and engaging stories.

In the next chapter, we will look at another essential journalistic technique: the interview. You'll see best practices for identifying and preparing sources, conducting the interview, and turning it all into rich content.

I hope you understand the power of storytelling and are already thinking about how to apply these narrative techniques to your own content. Don't forget the classic elements of a good story.

Remember: facts you can find anywhere, but captivating stories capture people's minds and hearts. Invest in creative narratives and inspire your audience.

INTERVIEWS AND RELIABLE SOURCES

In previous chapters, you saw the importance of applying journalistic techniques to content marketing, including storytelling and captivating narratives.

Now it's time to explore another essential strategy from journalism: interviewing experienced and reliable sources.

In this chapter, you'll see how to identify and prepare good sources, conduct engaging interviews, and turn it all into rich content for your audience.

Ready to dominate interviews? So let's start!

THE IMPORTANCE OF INTERVIEWING EXPERTS

Before we get into practical tips, you need to understand why talking to experts and opinion leaders is so valuable for content marketing.

Some of the main reasons for conducting interviews are:

- Offers exclusive insights your audience can't find elsewhere

- Human and captivating, connects your audience with respected experts

- Reinforces your authority by being with influential figures

- Saves research time and generates ideas for new content

- Can be reused in different formats: text, audio, video, etc.

- Easier to rank in search engines as it contains original content

As you can see, interviews have unique benefits for both you and your audience. Therefore, it is a type of content that every content creator must master.

WHERE TO FIND GOOD INTERVIEWEES

Now that you know the importance of interviewing, where do you find the best experts to talk to? Here are some suggestions:

- Influencers in your niche on social media

- Authors of popular books related to your topic

- Executives from relevant companies in your sector

- Teachers and academic researchers

- Leaders of large communities, groups and forums

- Journalists who cover your segment

- Speakers at events, meetups and conferences

- Podcasters who discuss aligned topics

The ideal is to combine very influential people, who will bring authority, with other names that are not yet known, who will help you gain prominence.

And don't be afraid to talk to names outside your niche, too. Sometimes a look from another area brings unexpected insights.

PREPARING THE GROUND FOR THE INTERVIEW

After selecting the interviewees, it's time to prepare the ground for the conversation to flow in the best way.

First, explain about yourself, your work and the objectives of the interview. Make the person comfortable and interested in participating.

Then, anticipate some questions and the main topics you want to explore. But leave the conversation open to delve deeper into insights that arise at the time.

Research a lot about the person's background and ideas, to ask more in-depth questions and establish a personal connection during the conversation.

And don't forget the practical aspects: define the best channel (in-person, video call, etc.), time, date, expected duration, necessary equipment and whether you can record and publish the interview.

TYPES OF QUESTIONS FOR A GREAT INTERVIEW

During the interview itself, it's essential to ask the right types of questions to extract the most valuable insights.

Some examples:

- Open: ask for more details and explanations. Ex: What are the biggest challenges of...?

- Closed: direct answers, often just "yes" or "no". Great for confirming data and facts.

- Funnel: starts comprehensively and focuses on the main theme. Explores topics from multiple perspectives.

- Deepening: they ask for more details about something already answered. Ex: Can you talk more about...?

- Hypothetical: proposes imaginary scenarios to stimulate interesting insights.

- Challenging: puts the person's beliefs to the test. The ideal is to do it at the end, when you are already comfortable.

- Personal: reveal motivations, stories, weaknesses and learnings of the interviewee. Humanize the conversation.

Switch between these types to make the conversation dynamic and explore the topic in depth, from practical experience to subjective aspects.

CONDUCTING THE INTERVIEW

During the conversation itself, pay attention to body language and reactions to direct the interview in the best way:

- Take notes on key points and in-depth questions to explore more at the right time.

- Don't interrupt too much, but don't be afraid of silence.

Wait for the person to completely finish their idea before asking a new question.

- Maintain eye contact, nod positively and show interest in what is being said.

- If the person rambles a lot, bring the focus back to the main topic with leading questions.

- Be prepared to improvise and change the direction of the conversation if interesting unplanned insights arise.

With empathy and practice, you will develop the ideal way to conduct captivating and productive interviews.

TRANSFORMING THE INTERVIEW INTO CONTENT

After finishing the interview, one of the most important parts arrives: transforming that conversation into valuable content for your audience.

For texts and podcasts, select key insights and produce a script with a clear beginning, middle and end.

In video, edit the best excerpts and add extra scenes to illustrate the most important points of the conversation.

If you are going to publish the full interview, produce a description and highlights of the topics covered to guide the audience.

If you want to turn it into smaller articles, break the interview into parts organized by subject or question.

The ideal is to generate as much content as possible from an interview. Test different formats and angles.

So a 30-minute conversation can easily lead to a podcast special, blog articles, social media excerpts, and more.

And don't forget to invite the interviewee to share this interview with their own audience. This helps expand reach.

With experience, you will become an expert in getting the most out of every minute of conversation with experts.

STRATEGIES TO STAND OUT IN THE WORLD OF PODCASTS

Have you ever thought about venturing into the world of podcasts and audio interviews? Here are some powerful tips:

- Invest in professional audio equipment to record conversations with high quality.

- Have a flexible script, but make occasional edits later to maintain only the best content.

- Compose a striking sound identity, with personalized vignettes, tracks, etc.

- Advertise your podcast on all platforms: Spotify, Apple Podcasts, etc.

- Intersperse solo episodes with interviews to vary the formats.

- Create extra content on YouTube and social media to promote the episodes.

- Improve your podcast art and descriptions to attract new listeners.

With consistency, creativity and good interviews, your podcast can become a very powerful content platform for your business.

IT'S TIME TO GET YOUR HANDS DRINKING!

We reach the end of this chapter with a complete view on how to conduct engaging interviews and transform them into strategic content.

You've seen where to find good interviewees, how to prepare, what types of questions to ask, and how to lead a productive conversation that generates valuable insights.

Additionally, you learned how to transform these interviews into text, audio and video content to engage your audience.

Now it's time to put these lessons into practice! In the next chapter, we will go into another pillar of journalism: investigation and in-depth investigation into a topic.

I hope you understand the value of interviews to produce exclusive and strategic content. Find generous experts and generate insights your audience can't get elsewhere.

Remember: well-conducted interviews gain authority, engagement and new ideas for you. So get to work on this new format!

INVESTIGATION AND RESEARCH

In previous chapters, you learned essential journalistic techniques like storytelling and interviews to create engaging content.

The time has come to explore another crucial element: investigation and in-depth research into a topic.

In this chapter, we'll look at how to delve deeper into topics in your niche and present new perspectives and insights that your audience won't find elsewhere. Let's go on this journey?

THE IMPORTANCE OF RESEARCH IN JOURNALISM

First of all, why is investigation so important in traditional journalism? What benefits does it bring to the public?

Some of the main ones are:

- Reveals new facts and angles that were hidden

- Brings transparency and exposes problems that need attention

- Empowers citizens with reliable and impartial information

- Assists in decision making based on accurate data

- Allows you to check statements and speeches by powerful figures

- Combat misinformation with concrete sources and evidence

These elements are crucial to maintaining a free and well-informed society. And in content marketing, research also has great value.

THE POWER OF CONTENT INVESTIGATION

Well-done research demonstrates that you fully master your topic and go beyond superficial knowledge.

By doing in-depth research into a topic and presenting new perspectives, you become an authority in the niche.

Furthermore, insights that no one else presents generate curiosity and engagement. People love discovering things that were previously unknown.

Another benefit is providing more context and understanding about a complex topic. Clarifying frequent doubts with accurate data is also a way of investigating.

In other words, applying journalistic investigation techniques to your content brings credibility, interest and in-depth understanding to your audience.

SOURCES FOR RELIABLE INVESTIGATION

Now that you know its importance, how can you carry out a well-founded investigation into content marketing? What are the best fonts?

Some recommendations are:

- Interview multiple experts with different views.

- Research in-depth academic and scientific studies.

- Analyze raw data from surveys and public reports.

- Seek insights from professionals who work directly on the topic.

- Discover statistics and projections from renowned institutes.

- Consult regulations, laws and official documents.

- Verify statements and facts against other reliable sources.

- Make formal requests for information from public bodies.

The more sources you triangulate, the more accurate the conclusions of your investigation will be. Data that is repeated across multiple sources is more reliable.

TOOLS TO INVESTIGATE ONLINE

In addition to these human sources, there are also tools available online that facilitate remote investigation.

Some very useful examples:

- **Google Alerts** [21]: allows you to receive notifications whenever a specific term is mentioned on the internet. It's a great tool for monitoring a brand or topic's online presence.

- **BuzzSumo** [22]: helps you discover popular content on a specific topic. It's useful for understanding which topics are generating the most interest.

- **SEMrush** [23]: provides traffic and SEO data from competitor websites, which can be valuable for digital marketing strategies.

- **SimilarWeb** [24]: offers analysis of website and app metrics, helping you understand the performance and reach of a website or app.

- **Google Trends** [25]: shows popular searches and interest in topics over time, which can be useful for identifying trends.

- **Google Scholar** [26]: is a search tool that allows access to research and complete academic journals.

-Twitter **Advanced Search** [27]: Allows advanced search within Twitter, which can be useful for finding specific tweets or understanding what is being said about a specific topic on Twitter.

Using these tools combined with human sources allows you to explore a topic from different angles and gain more complete insights.

CREATIVE ANGLES TO INVESTIGATE

Find original angles to explore an already familiar theme. Some creative ideas:

- Investigate the same phenomenon in different places or cultures.

- Analyze the historical evolution of a trend over time.

- Discover the behind the scenes and the "whys" behind important decisions.

- Identify patterns and correlations between seemingly disconnected data.

- Understand the problem through the personal stories of those who were affected by it.

- Demystify popular beliefs with concrete evidence.

- Compare cases of success and failure within the same industry.

- Hear informed opinions outside your immediate circle.

Finding a new approach to something old or expanding into little explored areas are good strategies.

TELL HUMAN STORIES BEHIND THE FACTS

Also remember the importance of storytelling in these investigations. Combine hard data with human stories and practical examples.

By interviewing people with diverse experiences on the topic investigated, you obtain essential perspectives and experiences to illustrate this issue in practice.

Real stories make data come to life and help audiences put themselves in the shoes of those affected by the issue.

In addition to bringing new information to light, contextualize and show how it impacts people like your reader. The combination of proven facts, accurate data and captivating narratives is unbeatable.

TOOLS TO ORGANIZE YOUR INVESTIGATIVE PROCESS

Finally, how to organize and manage the entire investigation process? Some useful tools:

- **Trello** [28]: allows you to create boards to organize sources, data to check, schedules, etc.

- **Evernote** [29]: helps you save your notes with tags to find everything easily.

- **Google Docs** [30]: allows the production of collaborative drafts in real time.

- **Dropbox Paper** [31]: offers the ability to edit text, images and files in an organized way.

- **Grammarly** [32]: helps correct grammatical errors and improves the investigated text.

- **Otter.ai** [33]: offers the ability to automatically transcribe interviews.

These are some suggested tools to investigate like a reporter and produce in-depth content from scratch.

INVESTIGATE AND DEEPER INTO YOUR NICHE

We have reached the end of this chapter with complete tips for carrying out in-depth investigations in your niche like the great reporters.

You've seen the importance of going beyond superficial knowledge and the countless sources you can consult to support your insights.

Now it's your turn to find creative angles and bring new perspectives on topics in your sector. Combine facts, data, stories and online tools to create captivating and memorable investigations.

In the next chapter, we will see strategies for accurately calculating and analyzing data and statistics in content marketing.

I hope you understand the value of delving deeper into a relevant subject and becoming an investigative authority in your niche.

Remember: the more you discover, the more authority you gain. So get to work on this investigation and happy discovering!

DATA COLLECTION AND STATISTICS

In previous chapters, you saw the importance of carrying out in-depth investigations in content marketing.

The time has come to explore an essential facet of any investigation: the careful investigation of data and statistics.

In this chapter, you will see how to collect, analyze and present numbers accurately and strategically in your content. Here we go?

CREDIBILITY IS IN THE DETAILS

Why place so much emphasis on calculating metrics and statistics? What are the risks of citing data without adequate checking?

Some crucial reasons:

- Inaccurate numbers destroy your credibility as a reliable source.

- Important decisions are made based on accurate data.

- It is easy to distort and deceive using statistics out of context.

- Doubtful sources and unconscious biases can contaminate conclusions.

- False or distorted data becomes the basis for conspiracy theories.

Therefore, every serious professional carries out rigorous checks before publishing numbers and facts. This thorough investigation is what separates ethical journalism from misleading content.

WHERE TO LOOK FOR RELIABLE DATA

Now that you know the importance of analyzing data, what are the best sources for finding reliable statistics?

Some recommendations:

- Consolidated research institutes: Datafolha, IBGE and Ipea are well-established research institutes in Brazil.

-Government bodies: Ministries, Secretariats and regulatory agencies are government entities that exist in many countries, including Brazil.

- Peer-reviewed scientific publications: These are publications that undergo a rigorous review process by experts in the field before being published.

- Recognized banks and financial institutions: There are many banks and financial institutions recognized and regulated by the Central Bank of Brazil.

- Sector associations and professional councils: These are organizations that represent certain professions or industry sectors.

- Market analysis companies: Bloomberg and Morningstar are well-known companies that provide market analysis.

- Multilateral entities: The World Bank, IMF, UN and OECD are international organizations that work in various areas, including economic and social development.

Look for sources with proven credibility over time. And be aware of possible biases in private institutes or those with specific agendas.

Check out the methodology and sample

In addition to the source, before citing any data, check:

- How was the information collected? Survey, form, administrative data?

- Is the sample large and diverse enough to represent the population?

- What is the possible bias of the organization or author of the study?

- Is the data recent or outdated? Has any context changed since then?

- Is the methodology clear? How are categories defined?

These checks are valid even for reputable sources. Mistakes happen and methodologies can be questionable. Investigate with a critical eye.

BE CAREFUL WITH CONTEXT AND COMPARISONS

In addition to checking the origin and methodology, take care to present the data in the appropriate context.

Pay attention to details such as:

- The analyzed time interval. Monthly versus annual data can give very different impressions.

- The location or population profile of the sample. Generally, it cannot be extrapolated.

- Exceptions, variations and trends throughout the analyzed period.

- Definitions of metrics and what exactly they represent.

Also take special care with comparisons across studies, locations, and periods. Question:

- Are the collection methodologies similar enough to allow comparison?

- Do any definitions or categories differ between the compared data?

- Were the economic, social and demographic contexts similar in the comparisons?

- Are the periods comparable or are there large differences in intervals?

Avoid hasty comparisons that can lead the reader to misleading conclusions.

BEWARE OF SPURY CORRELATIONS

Another crucial point is not to confuse correlation with causality.

Observing that A occurs together with B does not mean that A causes B. There may be a hidden factor C causing both.

For example, obesity correlated with educational level. But the real cause could be income affecting both.

To prove causality, it is necessary to rigorously isolate variables through controlled experiments.

When in doubt, use terms like "association", "relationship" and "correlation" instead of stamping direct cause-and-effect relationships.

SIMPLIFY, BUT WITHOUT DISTORTING

You don't need to inundate the reader with endless tables of numbers. Simplify by presenting:

- The main conclusions directly.

- The key data that supports these conclusions.

- Examples and comparisons to give dimension and perspective.

- Be careful with percentages taken out of context. Prefer absolute numbers or clear rates.

- Well-constructed graphics are worth more than long paragraphs.

- But don't overdo the simplifications. Caveats and details matter.

ENGAGE THE READER WITH HUMAN INSIGHTS

Also remember the teachings on storytelling. Match numbers with human stories.

Look for reports from real people to exemplify how that data affects lives:

- The micro-entrepreneur whose business was affected by new regulations.

- The worker who suffered from a public policy cut.

- The family affected by a disease whose cases are increasing in the country.

Abstract data takes on another dimension when its concrete effects become evident. Never forget empathy.

USEFUL TOOLS IN DATA ANALYSIS

Finally, some useful tools for analyzing and simplifying data:

- **Microsoft Excel** [34]: It is an electronic spreadsheet tool that allows the organization, analysis of data and the creation of pivot tables to summarize large sets of data.

- **Google Sheets** [35]: It is an online spreadsheet tool that allows real-time collaboration and integrations with other tools.

- **Tableau** [36]: It is a data visualization tool that allows the creation of interactive analytical dashboards.

- **Power BI** [37]: It is a suite of business analysis tools that offers insights across your organization and allows you to create visual reports and personalized management dashboards.

TIME TO ANALYZE DATA LIKE A REPORTER

We come to the end of this chapter with comprehensive tips for collecting, checking, analyzing, and presenting data ethically and accurately.

You've seen reliable sources of statistics, common pitfalls with numbers, and the balance between simplifying and maintaining accuracy.

Now it's your turn to gather data to support your investigations and content. Find insights in numbers, but never forget the people behind them.

In the next chapter, we'll look at editing and proofreading strategies to refine and improve any content before publishing.

I hope you understand your responsibility when presenting numbers and are ready to crunch them like a true reporter.

Remember, credibility comes with expertise. Investigate, analyze and simplify data carefully and ethically. This is the basis of accurate journalism.

CONTENT EDITING AND REVIEW

In previous chapters, you learned about collecting and analyzing data to create reliable and informed content.

Now is the time to explore the final steps before publishing: editing and reviewing content.

In this chapter, we'll look at editorial principles, writing and proofreading tips to refine your content to perfection. Let's start?

THE IMPORTANCE OF EDITING

Why dedicate so much time to editing and proofreading? Why not publish as soon as the draft is ready?

Some crucial reasons:

- Removes inaccuracies, factual errors and inconsistencies.
- Improves the logical flow of ideas and structure.
- Eliminates deviations from the central focus or unnecessary sections.
- Ensures compliance with guidelines and good practices.
- Aligns terminology for internal coherence.
- Takes care of details such as grammar, spelling and punctuation.
- Adapts the tone and language to the target audience.

Editing removes rough edges and elevates content to a professional level of quality before publishing.

FUNDAMENTAL EDITORIAL PRINCIPLES

What are the fundamental principles that guide the work of a content editor?

- **Clarity** - ideas must be understandable to the target audience.

- **Coherence** - avoid contradictions and maintain a consistent line of reasoning.

- **Cohesion** - logical connections between sentences and paragraphs.

- **Conciseness** - preferring the right word instead of several. Eliminate what doesn't add up.

- **Contextualization** - explain technical concepts. Do not assume prior knowledge.

- **Consistency** - standardize terminology, names, acronyms throughout the text.

- **Credibility** - all information needs to be verifiable and well-founded.

Following these fundamental editorial principles greatly increases the quality of the final published content.

BEWARE OF DUPLICATION OF CONTENT

Another crucial aspect of editing is avoiding content duplication, also known as self-plagiarism.

Because repeating long texts or passages can generate problems such as:

- Penalty in search engines for non-original content.

- Public distrust, which expects new material.

- Violates copyright by publishing third-party content.

- Lack of coherence when mixing different sources and views.

The ideal is to create 100% original content for each new material published.

But some occasional references to previous work are expected to provide context and build your authority organically over time.

The balance lies in relying on previous work without repeating it in its entirety. Always produce new insights.

WRITING TIPS FOR FLUID CONTENT

In addition to these general principles, there are also good writing practices for creating fluid text.

Some tips:

- Choose paragraphs and sentences of varying lengths to give rhythm to your reading.

- Avoid unnecessary words that do not add relevant information.

- Be careful with the passive voice, which can make the text heavy. Prefer the active voice.

- Replace technical terms with simpler equivalents when possible.

- Highlight keywords with bold, italics and quotation marks where appropriate.

- Bulleted lists help break long texts into consumable topics.

Investing in variance, conciseness and simplicity makes your content much more attractive and easier for your audience to assimilate.

THE POWER OF HUMAN REVIEW

As useful as tools like spell checkers are, it's still essential to have human proofreaders review your content.

Why? Because only we, human beings, can clearly assess whether the content makes sense, sounds natural and is well structured.

Furthermore, grammatical and typing errors often go unnoticed by automatic tools.

Therefore, always review the content yourself at different times before publishing. And outsourcing the review to someone qualified also adds extra layers of improvement.

A good tip is reverse review: reading the content backwards, checking titles and script without the text, to have a critical view.

This meticulous work makes all the difference in the quality that the public perceives.

THE RIGHT RHYTHM OF REVISIONS

How many reviews and edits are really necessary before publishing content? Here are some guidelines:

- Large reviews: at least 2 rounds separated by a few days for a fresh perspective.

- Micro-revisions: do them quickly before each publication, even for content that has already been revised.

- Periodic reviews: update and improve old content that continues to generate value.

- Instant review: during creation, you can immediately improve excerpts and phrases.

Finding your own rhythm is important. Excessive edits indefinitely delay publication. On the other hand, publishing without proofreading generates serious errors.

Test and discover the ideal quantity for your flow, ensuring quality before publishing.

TOOLS TO SPEED UP REVIEWS

Finally, some tools that make reviewers' work easier:

- **Grammarly** [38]: Corrects grammar and spelling errors instantly.

- **Hemingway** [39]: Evaluates the complexity of reading and suggests simplifications.

- **Google Docs** [40]: Has built-in commenting and change tracking features.

- **Scribens** [41]: Corrects Portuguese and technical terms.

- **Wordtune** [42]: Automatically smoothes complex sentences.

- **Quillbot** [43]: Replaces words with sophisticated synonyms.

Invest time in reviewing, but use technology to your advantage to speed up this essential task.

IT'S TIME TO REVIEW YOUR OWN CREATIONS

We come to the end of this chapter with a complete look at editing and proofreading to take your content to the next level.

You saw editorial principles, writing tips, the importance of human review and tools to speed up work.

Now it's your turn to put these lessons into practice and make finishing and reviewing an indispensable part of your content creation process.

In the next chapter, we'll explore strategies for choosing the best topics and angles for each type of content from scratch.

I hope you understand the great impact that editing has on the quality perceived by the public. Take the time to review your drafts.

Remember: excellence is in the details. With patience and technique, you can refine any text to perfection.

CHOOSING RELEVANT TOPICS AND ANGLES

In previous chapters, you learned about editing and proofreading to improve the final quality of any content before publication.

Now it's time to address the initial phases: how to choose the best topics and define relevant angles to explore in each new content you create.

Follow this chapter to fully master the process of designing any content project from scratch. Let's start?

UNDERSTANDING YOUR AUDIENCE

Before deciding on which topics and approaches to create content, it is essential to deeply understand your target audience. Relevance comes from solving the pains and interests of the people you want to reach.

Therefore, periodically survey your readers to find out:

- Main questions and problems they face
- Objectives they seek when consuming your content
- Preferences for formats, length, tone of voice
- Topics and terms most searched for on your website/blog
- What works best and worst in your current content

With this information, you can identify gaps and opportunities to create content that truly interests your audience.

ALIGNING WITH YOUR BUSINESS GOALS

However, be careful: meeting the public's needs is only part of the equation. Your content also needs to support your overall marketing and business goals.

So consider how each new piece of content aligns with goals like:

- Attract qualified leads to your funnel
- Position your company as an authority in the niche

- Increase traffic to the website or social networks

- Convert visitors into leads and customers

- Increase sales of specific products or services

- Nurture and retain current customers

Finding topics at the intersection of your audience's interests and your business goals is ideal for creating winning content.

UNDERSTANDING YOUR PERSONAS

Another powerful technique is defining buyer personas, fictional profiles that represent your most important audience segments.

For each persona, detail elements such as:

- Demographic data: age, gender, location, profession, etc.

- Personality and typical behaviors

- Challenges and problems faced

- Objectives and motivators

- Insights into your brand and products

Then, evaluate which content would be most relevant and valuable specifically for each persona in the different states of the funnel.

This helps you target your content in a more personalized and strategic way.

SEARCH AND INTEREST TRENDS

Aligning content with popular search terms also enhances organic discovery. Therefore, periodically research:

- Most searched keywords in your niche

- FAQs on Google related to your topic

- Subjects gaining search volume recently

Tools like **Google Trends** [44], **Keyword Tool** [45], **Keyword planner** [46] and **Buzzsumo** [47] are excellent for this.

But be careful: prioritize consistent keywords with good search intent, not just passing fads.

Insights from these tools should direct, not entirely determine, your editorial choices. Substance is more important than buzzwords.

CREATIVE AND CONTRASTING ANGLES

For already known topics, it is worth investing in creative and little explored angles. Some ideas:

- Treat a serious topic with humor and lightness

- Bring diverse and marginalized voices

- Make connections between non-obvious subjects

- Analyze a phenomenon from a new perspective

- Teach a complex skill in a simple way

- Demystify or deconstruct ideas made about something

Surprise, find new aspects, bring representation. This keeps the topics interesting.

USER JOURNEY AS A COMPASS

And always remember that content exists to guide the user on a journey that leads to conversion. Therefore, focus on topics that:

- Generate awareness and initial interest in your product or service

- Resolve key pain points and objections during consideration

- Facilitate and speed up the purchasing decision at the right time

- Increase post-sales retention and satisfaction

Each phase requires different approaches and content formats. Attracting is not the same as nurturing. Always consider where each persona is in the funnel.

PRIORITIZING QUALITY OVER QUANTITY

And speaking of formats, remember that less is more. Invest your time creating some extremely useful and well-produced content, instead of trying to produce superficial dozens.

Some criteria for prioritizing topics are:

- Alignment with your strategic goals

- Likelihood of generating engagement and conversions

- Perceived gap between content supply and demand

- Production feasibility considering deadlines and resources

- Potential to reach and impact many people

- Ability to be amplified via paid promotion

Always balancing these aspects - relevance, potential impact, feasibility - you spend your resources on content that will bring the most concrete ROI.

KEEPING A LONG-TERM VISION

And finally, remember that cultivating a loyal and engaged audience takes time. Your content needs to be part of your audience's regular information diet.

So invest in a consistent, long-term strategy, not just short-term tactics. Plan your content with an editorial vision, not just a promotional one.

By adopting this mentality as a trusted media outlet and not just a showcase for promotions, your audience will consume your content naturally along the way.

IT'S TIME TO DEFINE YOUR NEXT BIG THEMES

We reach the end of this chapter with a complete view on how to evaluate opportunities and choose the best topics and approaches for each new content investment.

You saw the importance of balancing audience interests, your business goals, search trends, creative insights and more during this curation.

Now it's your turn to put these lessons into practice and make sound editorial decisions to create a library of truly relevant and engaging content.

In the next chapter, we will see the importance of catchy titles and effective calls to action to increase interest in each piece of content.

I hope you understand that choosing good themes and angles already greatly INFLUENCES the final success of any content. Dedicate time to getting this first step right.

Remember: quality trumps quantity. Invest in planning to publish the right content, not just more content.

ENGAGING THE AUDIENCE WITH CAPTIVING TITLES

In previous chapters, you learned how to choose the best topics and approaches to create content that your audience actually wants to consume.

Now it's time to understand how to write a good title and call for each piece of content, in order to generate more clicks, views and engagement with your audience.

Follow this chapter to master the art of catchy titles. Let's start?

WHY THE TITLE IS CRUCIAL

Before we talk about how to create good titles, it's important to understand why they are so crucial to the success of any content. Some key reasons:

- The title is the first point of contact when the user finds your content.

- A weak title may make the user not even click and give it a chance.

- A strong title generates curiosity and interest in finding out more.

- Titles appear in search results and social networks, influencing clicks.

- A memorable title helps position you as an expert on the subject.

Given this importance, it is worth investing time and creativity to develop the best titles possible for each piece of content.

WHAT MAKES AN EFFECTIVE TITLE

Now that you know the importance of the title, what makes it effective? What elements cannot be missing?

Some of the main ones are:

- Make it clear what the content is about (theme/main focus)

- Be specific and direct, not vague or generic

- Evoke emotion or use an intriguing hook

- Speak directly to the reader when possible (You, Yours)

- Have relevant keywords combined with creative terms

- Be concise, typically between 60-80 characters

- Call the reader to action (verb in imperative)

Let's explore some techniques and examples for mastering these elements.

TYPES OF EFFECTIVE SECURITIES

There are some established title formats that deliver these elements well:

- List:
    "10 tips to become an inspiring leader"

- Question:
    "How much does it really cost to create an app?"

- Imperative (order):
    "Invest in stocks soon: definitive guide for beginners"

- Quote:
    "As Sonia Hess says, 'dreams move the world'"

- Shock/Provocation:
    "Experts warn: artificial intelligence will replace half of jobs in 5 years"

- Result/Benefit:
    "Learn to negotiate and double your salary in one year"

As you can see, more direct headings, with strong verbs, speak better to the reader and motivate action.

CONSECRATED FORMULAS

classic "formulas" for titles that just work:

- X reasons for Y
- The definitive guide to X
- X secrets about Y
- How to do X in X steps
- The fatal error that sank
- X things you didn't know about Y
- The best tips for X
- X questions about Y answered

Where X is your theme or keyword and Y is your focus or promise to the reader.

Test creative combinations of these time-honored structures to create interesting titles.

POWERFUL WORDS

Some examples of words commonly used in catchy titles:

- Surprising
- Curious
- Shocking
- Controversial
- Unexpected
- Extraordinary
- Incredible
- Comic

- Exclusive

These emotionally charged words help draw attention and generate interest in the content. Try using one of them at the beginning of the title.

INTRIGUING NUMBERS

Including numbers also works well, as it causes curiosity and surprise:

- 10 books that Bill Gates thinks everyone should read

- 7 morning habits of highly productive CEOs

- Learn English in 30 days with this simple method

- Study the 5 best investments for 2023

Numbers generate curiosity and a feeling of more concrete content. Use them wisely.

TO THE READER, ALWAYS

Also remember to speak directly to the reader whenever possible:

- Are you hydrating properly? Learn now

- Transform your career with this online course

- Watch your balance grow with these 5 investment tips

Titles aimed at "you" generate more engagement and a sense of practical usefulness of the content.

A/B TESTING

A good tip is to test different title options for the same content and see which generates the most clicks and engagement.

This can be done manually or with A/B testing tools integrated into blogs and websites.

This continuous learning through trial and error helps you create better and better titles.

BEWARE OF [48]DECEPTIVE CLICKBAITS

Finally, be careful not to fall into the temptation of clickbait , with false or exaggerated promises just to generate clicks.

This may work temporarily, but it destroys your credibility and trust with the public.

The ideal is to surprise, but always delivering what was promised.

Do you already know how to create powerful titles?

We come to the end of this chapter with a comprehensive look at catchy headlines and how they impact the success of your content.

You saw why they are crucial, elements of a good title, different formats and established formulas, as well as words and numbers that enhance results.

Now it's your turn to put these techniques into practice and raise the level of your titles. Good content with a weak title gets lost.

In the next chapter, we'll look at another essential element for generating engagement: effective calls to action.

I hope you understand the power that the title has to amplify results and are ready to improve yours.

Remember: a catchy title is half the battle. Invest time in this important gateway to your content.

THE INFLUENCE OF SOCIAL MEDIA ON CONTENT JOURNALISM

In previous chapters, you saw the importance of effective titles and calls to action to increase engagement with your content.

Now it's time to explore the impact of social media on journalism and content creation today.

In this chapter, you will understand how to adapt your content for better performance and engagement on digital platforms. Here we go?

THE REACH OF SOCIAL MEDIA

First, it's important to understand the massive reach of social media today.

According to Statista [49], as of October 2023, there are 5.3 billion internet users worldwide, which is equivalent to 65.7% of the global population. Of this total, 4.95 billion, or 61.4% of the world's population, were social media users. Also according to Statista [50], Instagram is one of the main social networks in the world, with 1.3 billion users (in terms of potential advertising reach). India is the country with the most Instagram users, with 229.55 million, followed by the United States (143.35 million), Brazil (113.5 million), Indonesia (89.15 million) and Turkey (48.65 million).

A survey carried out by Sortlist [51]estimates that internet users spend 145 minutes a day on social media. In Brazil, this time is even longer. Users spend around 3 hours and 45 minutes a day on social media, according to a study by Tracto [52].

It is clear that networks have become an essential platform for content distribution and cannot be ignored.

In addition to the huge audience, another crucial point is the speed with which viral content spreads on social networks nowadays.

This ease of rapid propagation allows your content to gain wide reach organically, if it manages to perform well on these platforms.

AUDIENCE CONTROL AND SEGMENTATION

Another huge benefit of social media is the ability to target and segment your content to specific audiences.

Each network has its particularities:

- **LinkedIn** [53]: focused on professionals and the B2B market.

- **TikTok** [54]: aimed at entertaining young audiences.

- **Instagram** [55]: popular among niche interests and influencers.

- **WhatsApp** [56]: used for direct communication and local connection.

- **Twitter** [57]: known for real-time news and debates.

- **Facebook** [58]: the most popular and comprehensive social network, with diverse resources such as groups, pages, events, marketplace [59], etc.

- **YouTube** [60]: a video platform for different types of content, such as music, education, humor, etc.

- **Reddit** [61]: an online forum for discussing various topics, organized into communities called subreddits.

- **Pinterest** [62]: a social network to share and discover creative ideas, such as crafts, decoration, fashion, etc.

- **Snapchat** [63]: a social network for sending and receiving photos and videos that disappear after a while, with fun filters and special effects.

You can customize the approach on networks according to each main audience. This increases engagement.

REAL-TIME MONITORING AND RESPONSE

Social networks also allow you to interact and respond to the public in real time. You can:

- Know exactly when and where your content is being consumed.

- Quickly measure what is working or not.

- Answer questions and get feedback from followers instantly.

- Track mentions, keeping your brand close.

This real-time monitoring potential helps you better understand your audience and quickly respond to their demands.

HUMANIZATION AND BRAND APPROACHMENT

Another great benefit is the ability to humanize your brand, showing the more personal side of your members on social media.

By giving a voice and image to those behind the company, your brands become more:

- **Friendly** : the public gets to know the real people behind the brand.

- **Accessible** : anyone can interact directly through networks.

- **Dynamic** : posts bring news, they are not static.

- **Authentic** : mistakes and the unique voice of each member are evident.

This all contributes to a more human and connected image, which is essential today.

NEW METRICS AND SUCCESS INDICATORS

Traditionally, the main indicators of journalism were the reach of distribution (subscribers, copies sold) and advertiser revenue.

On social media, new metrics come onto the scene, such as:

- Number of followers, subscribers, group members
- Engagement rate (likes, comments, shares)
- Views and content consumption time
- Traffic and leads originating from social media
- Sentiment and mentions on the web (positive, negative, neutral)

Therefore, you need to adapt the success criteria and optimize your content considering these new factors.

NEW OPPORTUNITIES AND CHALLENGES

Finally, social media has brought both new opportunities and challenges to modern journalism.

Some of the main ones:

- Democratization of information and plurality of voices
- Speed and ease of publication and distribution
- Greater interaction with the public
- New formats: threads, stories, livestreams

<!---->

- Shallow or exaggerated content to go viral
- Information bubbles and echo chambers
- Viral spread of misinformation as well
- Difficulty in monetizing content

It is up to modern content producers to know how to take advantage of opportunities and mitigate the risks and problems that arise in this new environment.

Are you ready for the future of content marketing?

We reach the end of this chapter with a comprehensive view of how social networks have transformed journalism and content creation today.

You understand the networks' huge audience, rapid viral spread, targeting potential, real-time monitoring and much more.

He also saw new challenges brought by this environment, which requires a solid ethical stance.

Now it's your turn to plan your content strategy considering these opportunities and adaptations to a scenario dominated by networks.

In the next chapter, we'll dive into another big content marketing trend: search engine content optimization, also known as SEO.

I hope you understand the crucial importance of social media for journalism and are ready to master this new field.

Remember: our job as content producers is to inform the public. Platforms may change, but the essence remains.

SEO AND KEYWORDS: THE PERFECT MARRIAGE

In previous chapters, we discussed the transformation brought by social networks to the creation and distribution of content.

Now it's time to explore another crucial content marketing trend: search engine content optimization, known as SEO.

In this chapter, you will see how to combine SEO and keywords to increase the reach and discoverability of your content. But...

Before getting into SEO tips, you need to understand how Google and other search engines rank results on the page.

There are more than 200 criteria, which include elements such as:

- Keywords in title, URL and text

- Page loading speed

- Time the user spends on the website (engagement metrics)

- Domain credibility and reputation

- Links received from other relevant websites

- Age of the domain and content (older tends to rank better)

- Use of multimedia and relevant visual elements

OPTIMIZING FOR YOUR KEY TERMS

A crucial point of SEO is choosing the right key terms to optimize each piece of content you create.

To do this, use tools like Google Keyword Planner and Google Trends to discover:

- Which terms are most searched for in your niche

- What type of intent does the search indicate (information, purchase, downloads, etc.)

- The search volume for each keyword

- The level of competitiveness to rank with each term

This will ensure you are optimizing for words that people actually use in their everyday lives.

ESSENTIAL SEO TECHNIQUES

Once you have selected key terms, apply these techniques to optimize each piece of content:

- Use the keyword in the title and URL

- Mention the word a few times in the text organically

- Highlight the word in bold or italics

- Include synonyms and variations of the keyword in the content

- Use HTML tags like H1 and H2 with the targeted terms

- Post well-optimized images and videos with alt texts

- Make the most of spaces like your website description to include key terms

When well applied in a relevant volume, these techniques greatly increase the ranking of content.

AUTHORITY ALSO COUNTS FOR A LOT

Also remember that site authority strongly influences your rankings. Therefore, some good practices are:

- Publish extensive and in-depth content, with unique and exclusive information

- Get links from relevant websites pointing to your content

- Invest in professional design and a pleasant user experience

- Have lots of content focused on niche keywords

The more you prove expertise on a topic, the better positions your content achieves over time. Authority is built content by content.

CONSTANTLY MONITOR AND TEST

And don't forget to track metrics such as ranking position, traffic from organic sources and keyword usage monthly.

Tools like Google Analytics [64], SEMRush [65] and Search Console [66] are valuable for this.

A/B testing also helps you understand which combination of title, meta description, and content works best for each keyword.

SEO, well applied, is a great ally in making your content findable and relevant in search engines. **Don't neglect it**.

Are you ready to start creating optimized content?

We come to the end of this chapter with a very solid overview of how to apply SEO alongside your content to maximize organic discovery.

You saw the importance of ranking well nowadays, the main factors that Google considers and several essential content optimization techniques.

Now it's your turn to put this learning into practice and start creating optimized and strategic content, ranking for your main key terms.

In the next chapter, we'll look at how to measure and track results to prove content marketing ROI.

I hope you understood the "perfect marriage" between quality content and SEO. Together, they enhance each other to bring your content to more people.

Remember: your content needs to be found to meet your goals. Include SEO in your planning.

MEASURING THE IMPACT AND SUCCESS OF CONTENT

In previous chapters, we discussed the importance of social media and SEO to boost the reach of content in search engines.

Now it's time to understand how to measure the impact of your content strategy and define what success really is in this context.

In this chapter, you'll see metrics, KPIs [67], and tools for tracking results and optimizing your content. Here we go?

WHY DOES MEASUREMENT MATTER?

Before we talk about how to measure, you need to understand why this is so important for content marketing today.

Some crucial reasons:

- Know what works to enhance these initiatives and cut out what does not generate value.

- Understand how your buyer personas respond to each format and channel.

- Identify bottlenecks in the funnel to optimize and increase conversions.

- Compare performance between different campaigns and periods.

- Justify investment in content with concrete data for leadership.

- Give objective insights for decision making based on facts, not just opinions.

It is clear that measuring results is essential to prove, optimize and expand your content strategy.

MAIN METRICS AND KPIS

Now that you know the importance of measuring, what are the main indicators and metrics to monitor?

Some of the most important:

- **Total reach** - views, impressions

- **Engagement** - clicks, comments, shares, subscriptions

- **Traffic** - total visits, unique visitors, pages/session

- **Conversions** - leads, sales generated, downloads, signups

- **Sentiment** - % of positive, negative and neutral mentions

- **Ranking** - position in searches for your key terms

- **ROI** - profit generated by leads/sales resulting from content

The ideal is to combine exposure, engagement, conversions and ROI metrics to have a complete picture.

ESSENTIAL ANALYSIS TOOLS

And what are the main tools for collecting and analyzing these content metrics?

Some of the most used:

- **Google Analytics** [68]- complete data on traffic, behavior, conversions

- **Google Search Console** [69]- ranking data and search performance

- **Buzzsumo** [70]- content performance by social network and engagement

-Facebook **Insights** [71]- metrics for Facebook pages and posts

-Twitter **Analytics** [72]- Twitter engagement data

- Google Data Studio [73]- consolidation of data from multiple sources into dashboards

Integrating these tools to have a unified view of the data is ideal for making well-informed decisions.

SUCCESS DOESN'T COME FROM NOTHING

Also remember that significant results take time and consistency. Just because a post goes viral doesn't mean your content as a whole is doing well.

Some reasonable **benchmarks** [74] are:

- 6 to 12 months to start gaining organic traction

- 10 to 20 posts to start ranking in some searches

- 200 to 300 subscribers to the list for every 1000 visitors

Be persistent and analyze trends over time, not just isolated data. Sustainable results take work.

SUCCESS DEPENDS ON YOUR GOALS

And speaking of results, remember that success can only be measured in relation to the objectives originally set.

Some fundamental questions:

- Is the content attracting your target audience?

- Is it generating qualified leads for the funnel?

- Are leads becoming customers after consuming your content?

- Is the ROI of the content positive considering creation/distribution costs?

- Has your brand's positioning improved in the public's mind?

Any metric only makes sense when compared to the KPIs and specific objectives previously outlined for that content program.

Start measuring what matters today

We reach the end of this chapter with a very solid view of why and how to effectively measure the impact and success of your content strategy.

You've seen the importance of establishing clear objectives and choosing aligned key metrics to collect the right data and derive valuable insights from your content.

Now it's time to put these lessons into practice and start measuring what really matters, making decisions based on the data collected.

In the next chapter, we'll talk about planning and organizing to have a consistent and sustainable long-term content strategy.

I hope you understand the crucial value of measurement to prove ROI and continually optimize your content marketing efforts. What is not measured cannot be managed.

Remember: well-used data brings insights. Define your KPIs and key metrics to get the most out of your content.

LONG-TERM CONTENT PLANNING

In previous chapters, you saw the importance of measuring results to extract insights and optimize your content strategy.

The time has come to explore how to plan and organize content creation consistently over the long term.

In this chapter, you'll see tools, practices, and principles for building a solid, sustainable content ecosystem. Here we go?

WHY IS PLANNING CRUCIAL?

Before we talk about how to plan, you need to understand why this process is so fundamental to success in content marketing.

Some main reasons:

- Ensures constancy, with new content being published periodically.

- Maximizes available resources, with production aligned with priorities.

- Allows you to view content gaps and opportunities in the macro.

- Facilitates execution, with content ready to go live.

- Ensures agility for adaptations based on data and insights.

- Aligns teams and collaborators in a common purpose.

Strategic planning is the key to building a rich and sustainable content ecosystem.

BASING YOUR PLAN ON INSIGHTS

Remember that your editorial plan should be guided by insights from your audience, not hunches.

Some fundamental sources:

- Data on best-selling/used products and services

- Insights from sales and service teams

- Surveys and feedback collected from customers

- Opinions and online reviews from users

- Content metrics and website traffic analysis

- Search trends and trending topics in the niche

The more data you have about your buyer personas, the better you can create a plan aligned to their needs.

TOOLS TO FACILITATE PLANNING

There are several online tools that can facilitate content planning and organization:

- **Trello** [75]- organizes your schedule and workflow into boards.

- **Asana** [76]- manages projects with tasks, deadlines and responsible parties.

- **Google Docs** [77]- collaborative document for brainstorming and collective construction of ideas.

- **Google Sheets** [78]- online spreadsheets to organize editorial calendars.

- **Excel** [79]- offline option for those who prefer a robust spreadsheet.

- **Canva** [80]- visually creates your schedule with ready-made posts and artwork.

Find the tools that work for your team and workflow to make this planning easier.

CONTENT TYPE

Also remember to align the plan with business objectives, creating specific content for each stage:

- **Top of the funnel:** content that generates awareness such as posts on social media, introductory ebooks, etc.

- **Middle of the funnel:** nourishing with materials that educate, such as guides, case studies, demonstrations, etc.

- **End of the funnel** : content that motivates action, such as webinars, white papers , free trials etc.

- **After-sales** : service, training, upselling with content for customers.

Your plan must have a good mix of content to move leads through all stages to purchase.

CONSISTENCY IS KEY

Also remember that consistency is key. Have new content go live at a constant frequency:

- Generates traffic and recurring qualified audience.

- Contributes to ranking by adding pages regularly.

- Creates the habit and relevance for your audience to return.

Always plan the next wave of content before even publishing the current one to maintain momentum.

EDITORIAL CALENDARS MAKE IT EASY

A very useful resource for consistent planning are editorial calendars with content mapped out in advance:

- Makes it easier to visualize the funnel and which stages require the most content.

- Allows prior preparation and parallel work on several fronts.

- Promotes alignment, with the entire team aware of what

will be published.

- Creates consistency in the distribution of formats over time.

The editorial calendar is a powerful tool for the sustained production of quality content.

EVERGREEN CONTENT BEYOND THE MOMENT

Within your planning, focus not only on content associated with the present moment, but also on evergreen materials, which continue to generate value in the long term.

Some examples of evergreen content:

- Step by step tutorials

- Lists of the best X

- Comparison between popular options

- Series on the fundamentals of an area

- Timeless case studies

- Deep reflections on a topic

This "shelf" content helps you build a rich library and collection that continues to attract leads.

ADAPT YOUR PLAN CONSTANTLY

Remember that your planning is not something fixed and immutable. Track metrics, trends, and audience insights to adapt your calendar regularly.

Some occasions that require adaptations:

- Changes in public demand and interests

- Launch of new products or features

- Exit or entry of important employees

- New opportunities such as partnerships or events

- Performance below expectations of some format or channel

Solid planning is essential, but flexibility is also key to optimizing efforts.

Ready to start planning your content?

We reach the end of this chapter with a complete overview of planning, organization and principles for having a solid content strategy.

You understood why planning is crucial, saw different tools that facilitate the process and techniques for building a rich and sustainable content ecosystem.

Now it's your turn to put this learning into action and start outlining your own strategic content plan for the entire year.

In the next chapter, we'll talk about efficient distribution to get your content to the widest possible reach.

I hope you understand that a good editorial plan is the foundation of any strong content strategy. Dedicate time to this.

Remember: consistent content builds authority. With a solid plan, you can produce in a strategic and sustained way.

CONTENT DISTRIBUTION STRATEGIES

In previous chapters, you saw the importance of planning to maintain a consistent and sustainable content strategy.

Now it's time to explore the next step: how to efficiently distribute and amplify your content to reach the largest audience possible.

In this chapter, we'll look at channels, platforms, techniques and best practices to maximize the reach and impact of your content. Here we go?

WHY DOES DISTRIBUTION MATTER?

Before we talk about channels and strategies, you need to understand why distribution makes all the difference to the success of your content.

Some main reasons:

- Well-distributed content reaches more people.

- Amplifies dividends from the investment already made in creation.

- Allows you to test channels and prioritize the best performing ones.

- Generates avidity and a sense of exclusivity with content reserved for subscribers.

- Value other vehicles that share your content.

A good distribution strategy enhances the reach, engagement and ROI of your content.

WHERE IS YOUR AUDIENCE?

Before defining where to distribute, map out where your target audience is actually consuming content:

- Social platforms: Instagram, YouTube, LinkedIn, TikTok?

- Segment forums and communities.

- Podcasts and other popular channels in the niche.

- Professional platforms like SlideShare and Medium.

- Relevant marketplaces: Amazon, Etsy, AppStore etc.

Distribute mainly on channels frequented by your audience to optimize efforts.

THE POWER OF YOUR OWN CHANNELS

Also remember to make the most of your own channels before seeking external amplification.

Some options are:

- Email marketing for subscriber base and leads.

- Pop-ups and push notifications on your website.

- Featured on the cover and strategic sections of your website.

- Facebook and Instagram Ads leveraging content that performs.

- Organic boost on networks promoting high quality posts.

Focus on getting the most out of your assets before looking for outsourced channels. This way you better control the user experience.

THE IMPORTANCE OF PUBLIC RELATIONS

Another powerful content distribution avenue that cannot be overlooked is traditional public relations.

Some interesting initiatives you can pursue:

- Press office to promote releases about your content to the media.

- Direct contact with journalists and vehicles in your niche presenting exclusive insights.

- Contributions of articles or comments as an expert for relevant vehicles.

- Interviews on podcasts, lives and other third-party platforms that add authority.

- Promotional partnerships with important players in your segment.

ANALYZE THE NEXT STEPS AFTER DISTRIBUTION

Another important aspect is to look beyond distribution and plan what to do next to generate new leads and sales.

Some options to maximize each new distribution:

- Direct link to your homepage or sales page.

- Form for capturing data and emails.

- Time-limited offer to capitalize on rising interest.

- Automated email sequence to nurture leads.

- Sponsored ads for remarketing .

Your content needs to be a ramp for next interactions and not an end in itself. Plan ahead.

AVOID SATURATION ON THE SAME NETWORKS

Also remember that there must be a balance between consistency and saturation.

Some important precautions:

- Don't post the same content on all networks at the same time. Spread it out throughout the week.

- Give it time to like and get engagement before distributing much more.

- Vary the formats, not just the post link. Image excerpts, quotes, statuses, etc.

Saturating your own networks and followers will generate fatigue and reduce reach. Find the ideal frequency.

KEEP YOUR DATA SAFE

And finally, never forget the security of your users' and subscribers' data when distributing content across multiple channels.

Some good practices:

- Integrate with email marketing and CRM systems to maintain control of data.

- Guide people to sign up on your website, not just social networks.

- Have very clear and up-to-date privacy policies.

- Do not share contact lists directly, use secure systems.

- Train your team on data protection laws like LGPD, CCPA, etc.

Protecting confidential information must be a top priority in any distribution strategy.

Ready to distribute your content widely?

We reach the end of this chapter with a complete view on efficient content distribution to maximize results.

You've seen the importance of mapping your audiences, leveraging your own channels, seeking public relations opportunities and much more.

Now it's your turn to put these strategies into practice and take your content to the greatest possible reach, converting as many leads as possible.

In the next chapter, we will make a general conclusion summarizing the main lessons and insights from this book.

I hope you understand the potential that multichannel distribution has to exponentially amplify the results of your content.

Remember: your content needs to be seen to generate impact. Invest time in distribution.

FINAL CONSIDERATIONS

We reach the final chapter of this book with a comprehensive journey on how to apply journalism techniques to content marketing.

Throughout the chapters, you've seen practical lessons and insights to master every step of content creation, from ideation to distribution.

We saw the importance of deeply understanding your target audience, defining good themes and creative angles, developing engaging narratives, conducting rich interviews, checking facts and data, planning strategically and much more.

You also learned about trends in modern journalism such as the rise of social networks, the importance of SEO and the new challenges brought by the digital environment.

We explore all the elements that allow you, the content producer, to create informative and captivating materials that generate real value for your audience and support your business objectives.

I hope you made good use of all the practical suggestions along the way. More than simple theory, this book sought to give concrete examples of how to apply each principle.

Now it's your turn to put this learning into action and take your content to a new level. I trust that you come away from this reading much more prepared to plan, research, write, review, promote and distribute winning content.

Always remember that producing content that matters requires a powerful combination of journalistic technique and marketing strategy. And you now master these two areas.

So don't waste any more time. Start creating your next content now, keeping in mind everything you learned on these pages.

Plan in advance, gather information, build engaging narratives, take care of editing, invest in effective titles, measure results and distribute widely.

By putting into practice the techniques taught here, I'm sure you'll see your leads, sales and authority grow gradually over time.

Content marketing, when done masterfully and consistently, delivers concrete results like no other inbound marketing strategy.

So it's up to you now to take advantage of this potential. Go ahead and inform, educate, entertain and win over your target audience with your best version of marketing journalism.

Thank you very much for accompanying me on this journey so far. I hope this book inspires you to take your content to new heights of quality and excellence. I'm counting on you to spread these techniques even further and positively transform our digital world.

A big hug and much success!

READING SUGGESTION

ASSAD, Nancy.
Content marketing: how to make your company take off in digital media.

BACKLINK.
On Page SEO: The Definitive Guide.

BOUNEGRU, Liliana et al.
The Data Journalism Handbook 2: Towards a Critical Data Practice.

BUSSAB, Wilton de O.; MORETTIN, Pedro.
Basic Statistics.

CAIRO, Alberto.
How charts lie: getting smarter about visual information.

CANAVILHAS, João.
Web journalism : 7 characteristics that make the difference.

CONTENT MARKETING INSTITUTE.
B2B Content Marketing Benchmarks, Budgets and Trends.

DAVIS, Denise.
Get to the Point! Sharpen Your Message and Make Your Words Matter.

GROBEL, Lawrence.
The art of the interview: lessons from a master of the craft.

EINSOHN, Amy.
The Copyeditor's Handbook: A Guide for Book Publishing and Corporate Communications.

FISHKIN, Rand; HØGENHAVEN, Thomas.
Inbound Marketing and SEO: Insights from the Moz Blog.

GILAD, Suzanne.
Copyediting and Proofreading For Dummies.

GOMES, Wilson.

Journalism, facts and interests: essays on journalism theory.

GRAY, Jonathan; CHAMBERS, Lucy; BOUNEGRU, Liliana.
The data journalism handbook: how journalists can use data to improve the news.

HALVORSON, Kristina; RACH, Melissa.
Content Strategy for the Web.

HERMIDA, Alfred.
Tell Everyone: Why We Share and Why It Matters.

HOUSTON, Brant.
The investigative reporter's handbook: a guide to documents, databases and techniques.

JUDD, Karen.
Copyediting: a practical guide.

KAUSHIK, Avinash.
Web analytics 2.0: the art of online accountability and science of customer centricity.

KOTLER, P.; KARTAJAYA, H.; SETIAWAN, I.
Marketing 4.0: from traditional to digital.

KRUG, Steve.
Don't Make Me Think, Revisited: A Common Sense Approach to Web Usability.

LAGE, Nilson.
Theory and technique of reporting, interviewing and journalistic research.

LIEB, Rebecca.
Content Chemistry: The Illustrated Handbook for Content Marketing.

PULIZZI, Joe.
Epic Content Marketing: How to Tell a Different Story, Break through the Clutter, and Win More Customers by Marketing Less.

PULIZZI, Joe; BARRET, Newt.
Get content get customers: turn prospects into buyers with content marketing.

REED, James.
101 Interview Questions You'll Never Fear Again.

RENO, Denis; FLORES, Jesus.
Transmedia journalism : multiple perspectives.

ROCKLEY, Ann; COOPER, Charles.
Managing Enterprise Content: A Unified Content Strategy.

ROSE, Robert; PULIZZI, Joe.
Killing Marketing: How Innovative Businesses Are Turning Marketing Cost Into Profit.

ROSE, Robert; PULIZZI, Joe.
Managing Content Marketing: The Real-World Guide for Creating Passionate Subscribers to Your Brand.

SIMMONDS, Ross.
The Content Distribution Playbook.

SOUZA, Alceu et al.
Accuracy and precision: reviewing concepts accurately.

TRAQUINA, Nelson.
Journalism theories: why the news is the way it is.

WEINBERG, Tamar.
The new community rules: marketing on the social web.

As we turn the final page of this journey together, I sincerely hope that the learnings shared here have touched your heart and sparked new perspectives. If this book has brought you any value, I kindly ask that you take a few moments to leave a review on Amazon. Your words not only help me grow and hone my craft, but they also guide other readers in their quests for knowledge and inspiration. Your opinion is a valuable gift, both for me and for the community of readers looking for stories that transform. I sincerely thank you for sharing this journey with me and I hope we can meet again in the pages of a new adventure.

REGINALDO OSNILDO

Hello, I'm Reginaldo Osnildo, author and innovator in the areas of sales, technology, and communication strategies. My experience ranges from the academic environment, as a professor and researcher at the University of Southern Santa Catarina, to practice as a strategist at Grupo Catarinense de Rádios. With a PhD in sales narratives and digital convergence, and a master's degree in storytelling and social imaginary, I bring my readers a unique fusion of theory and practice. My goal is to provide knowledge in a simple, practical and didactic language, encouraging direct application in personal and professional life.

Yours sincerely

Reginaldo Osnildo

+55 48 991913865

reginaldoosnildo@gmail.com

---

[1] **Content marketing** refers to the strategy of creating, publishing, and distributing relevant, valuable, and consistent content to attract and retain a clearly defined target audience. The production of quality journalistic content, such as articles, news, analyzes and reports, can be a powerful tool for engaging audiences, building trust and authority, as well as educating and entertaining the public. The journalistic ability to tell stories in an engaging and informative way can be used to create content that not only promotes products or services, but also offers genuine value to the audience, establishing a deeper and lasting connection.

[2] **SEO**, or Search engine Optimization refers to the set of strategies and techniques applied to optimize content in order to improve its visibility in search engine results, such as Google. Journalistic techniques focused on content marketing often benefit from SEO practices to ensure that content is easily found by users when they search for certain topics. This involves carefully choosing relevant keywords, optimizing titles, meta descriptions and structuring content to meet search engine algorithms, providing greater reach and visibility for journalistic pieces produced for content marketing.

[3] **Phygital** is a term that combines "physical" and "digital", referring to the integration or fusion of physical and digital experiences. In the context of content marketing, the concept of "phygital" can be applied to create strategies that unite the physical and digital worlds. For example, content journalism that integrates physical elements, such as events or printed magazines, with digital components, such as online content or interactions on social networks, seeking a unified experience for the target audience. This may involve creating journalistic content that is not only consumed online, but also promotes physical events or tangible products, creating a comprehensive and engaging experience for the consumer.

[4] **Leads** are potential customers who have shown interest in a company's products or services. In the context of content marketing, journalistic techniques have the power to attract leads by offering valuable and relevant content to the audience. When a reader accesses an article, watches a video or interacts with any form of journalistic content created with a marketing focus, and expresses interest by providing contact information, such as email or filling out a form, they become a lead. Using effective journalistic techniques to produce attractive and informative content is essential for generating quality leads, which can later be nurtured and converted into customers.

[5] **ROI**, or Return on Investment, is a metric that evaluates the effectiveness and success of investments, comparing the gain obtained with the cost of the investment. In the context of content marketing, understanding ROI is crucial to evaluating the performance of applied journalistic strategies. This involves analyzing the impact of the content produced, measuring how much it contributed to the company's marketing objectives, whether generating leads, increasing sales or strengthening brand recognition. Measuring ROI helps determine which strategies and types of journalistic content are most effective, allowing adjustments and optimizations to maximize the return on the investment made in creating this material.

[6] **You can learn more about Moz by accessing this link** : https://www.safalta.com/online-digital-marketing/projects-case-studies/case-study-how-moz-overcame-challenges-to-build-a-content-marketing-strategy

[7] **You can access Moz's *Ultimate Guide to Content Planning* with this link** : https://moz.com/blog/the-ultimate-guide-to-content-planning

[8] **Millennials** are the generation born roughly between the early 1980s and mid-1990s. In the context of content marketing and journalistic techniques to boost this field, **millennials** represent a significant portion of the target audience. They are known for having a strong appetite for digital content, consuming news and information through online and social platforms. Journalistic strategies for content marketing often focus on attracting this generation by adapting the format and tone of content to suit their preferences, such as visual content, authentic messaging and interactive engagement. Understanding the interests, values and behaviors of millennials is essential when producing journalistic content to reach and engage this audience.

[9] **Buzz** refers to the excitement or interest generated around something, be it a product, event, idea or trend. In the context of content marketing, well-applied journalistic techniques can create a " buzz " around a specific topic. This occurs when the content produced arouses curiosity, engagement and discussions among the target audience, leading to a significant increase in the visibility and propagation of this content. Journalism's ability to create engaging and relevant narratives that spark interest and encourage sharing contributes to generating that " buzz " around a topic, product or service, driving awareness and reach of content marketing.

[10] **Hashtags** are words or phrases preceded by the "#" symbol (known as "tic-tac-toe"), used on social networks to categorize content and make it easily findable by other users interested in the same topic. In the context of content marketing and journalistic techniques, the strategic use of hashtags can amplify the visibility of content. By adding relevant hashtags to articles, posts or news materials, content creators make it easier for people interested in the topic to discover that material. This helps to expand the reach of the content and connect with the target audience, especially on social media, where hashtags are used as a mechanism for organizing and discovering content.

[11] **Feedback** is the response, evaluation or opinion offered about a product, service or performance. In the context of content marketing and journalistic techniques, feedback plays a crucial role. After publishing journalistic content for marketing, receiving feedback from readers or viewers is essential to understanding the effectiveness of the material. This feedback allows you to adjust and improve future content, adapting to the audience's preferences and interests, improving the quality and relevance of what is offered. Feedback can come from comments, shares, engagement metrics (such as time spent on page, click-through rates) and even direct consumer surveys, providing valuable information to improve and optimize marketing-oriented journalistic content strategies.

[12] You can learn more about the campaign at this link: https://www.shiftcomm.com/insights/big-mac-atm-case-study-going-viral/

[13] You can follow the case studies at this link: https://contently.com/case-studies/

[14] Forleo 's YouTube at this link: https://www.youtube.com/@marieforleo

[15] You can access Neil Patel's blog at this link: https://neilpatel.com/

[16] You can access the data at this link: https://ahrefs.com/blog/content-marketing-statistics/

[17] **To the *Buyer personas*** are fictional, detailed representations of a company's ideal customer. They are created based on demographic, behavioral and psychographic data, and aim to help marketing teams better understand their target audience. In the context of content marketing and journalistic techniques, creating content targeted at " buyer personas" is essential. Content marketing journalism can be shaped to meet personas' specific needs, interests and challenges, ensuring content is relevant and engaging for the desired target audience. By understanding " buyer personas", content creators can adapt journalistic approaches to effectively meet the ideal customer's needs and expectations.

[18] **Calls I'm Action (CTAs)** are strategic elements in content that encourage readers, viewers or listeners to take a specific action. In the context of content marketing and journalistic techniques, CTAs are essential for directing audience engagement towards desired objectives. These calls to action can range from requesting to share content on social media, subscribing to newsletters, to participating in surveys or converting into customers through links to products or services. In content journalism for marketing, the strategic inclusion of CTAs can guide the reader to the desired next step, whether to explore more content, interact on social media, or even convert into a lead or customer. Effective use of CTAs helps optimize the user journey by directing target audiences to specific actions that contribute to overall marketing objectives.

[19] **Storytelling** , or the art of telling stories, is a powerful technique. It involves creating and telling engaging narratives to communicate messages in a memorable and impactful way. By incorporating storytelling techniques into content marketing, professionals can transform dry information into captivating narratives. This not only keeps the audience interested but also creates an emotional connection. Well-constructed narratives can highlight the authenticity of the brand, convey values, solve public problems and, at the same time, entertain and educate. Storytelling in content marketing allows stories to become a bridge between the brand message and the consumer experience. Incorporating narrative elements into journalistic pieces can increase the effectiveness of the content, making it more memorable and impactful for the target audience.

[20] **Churn** refers to the customer turnover rate, that is, the rate at which customers stop using a company's products or services in a given period of time. In the context of content marketing, reducing churn rate is an important objective, as it indicates greater customer retention. Journalistic techniques in content marketing can play a role in reducing churn rate by creating continuous and relevant content. Quality content that keeps customers informed, engaged and satisfied can contribute to a positive experience, encouraging brand loyalty. By addressing customers' ever-evolving needs and interests through journalistic content, companies can maintain a long-lasting relationship, thereby reducing the churn rate .

[21] You can access the website at this link: https://www.google.com.br/alerts

[22] You can access the website at this link: https://buzzsumo.com/

[23] You can access the website at this link: https://pt.semrush.com/

[24] You can access the website at this link: https://www.similarweb.com/pt/

[25] You can access the website at this link: https://trends.google.com.br/trends/

[26] You can access the website at this link: https://scholar.google.com/

[27] You can access the website at this link: https://help.twitter.com/pt/using-x/x-advanced-search

[28] You can access the website at this link: https://trello.com/pt-BR

[29] You can access the website at this link: https://evernote.com/intl/pt-br

[30] You can access the website at this link: https://docs.google.com/

[31] You can access the website at this link: https://www.dropbox.com/pt_BR/paper

[32] You can access the website at this link: https://www.grammarly.com/

[33] You can access the website at this link: https://otter.ai/

[34] You can access the website at this link: https://www.microsoft.com/pt-br/microsoft-365/excel

[35] You can access the website at this link: https://www.google.com/intl/pt-BR/sheets/about/

[36] You can access the website at this link: https://www.tableau.com/pt-br

[37] You can access the website at this link: https://powerbi.microsoft.com/pt-br/

[38] You can access the website at this link: https://www.grammarly.com/

[39] You can access the website at this link: https://hemingwayapp.com/

[40] You can access the website at this link: https://docs.google.com/

[41] You can access the website at this link: https://www.scribens.com/

[42] You can access the website at this link: https://app.wordtune.com/

[43] You can access the website at this link: https://quillbot.com/

[44] You can access the website at this link: https://trends.google.com.br/trends/

[45] You can access the website at this link: https://keywordtool.io/pt

[46] You can access the website at this link: https://ads.google.com/intl/pt-BR_br/home/tools/keyword-planner/

[47] You can access the website at this link: https://buzzsumo.com/

[48] **Clickbaits** refer to sensationalist or deceptive techniques of presenting content online with the aim of attracting clicks, often at the expense of the content's actual accuracy or relevance. While the main goal of content marketing is to attract audience attention, it is crucial to maintain journalistic integrity by offering accurate and valuable information. Clickbait strategies can result in high click-through rates, but they often lead to a poor user experience as the content often does not meet the expectations created by the headline or headline.

[49] You can access the data at this link: https://www.statista.com/statistics/617136/digital-population-worldwide/

[50] You can access the data at this link: https://www.statista.com/statistics/578364/countries-with-most-instagram-users/

[51] You can access the data at this link: https://www.sortlist.com/datahub/reports/your-digital-year/

[52] You can access the data at this link: https://www.tracto.com.br/quanto-tempo-os-brasileiros-gastam-em-redes-sociais/

[53] To access LinkedIn, you can use the link www.linkedin.com . To access a specific profile, you can add /in/[username] to the end of the link.

[54] The official TikTok website can be accessed through the link www.tiktok.com .

[55] To access Instagram, you can use the link www.instagram.com . To access a specific profile, you can add /[username] to the end of the link.

[56] To create a direct link to a WhatsApp conversation with a specific number, you can use the format https://wa.me/<number>, replacing <number> with the desired phone number.

[57] The official Twitter (X) website can be accessed through the link www.twitter.com .

[58] To access Facebook, you can use the link www.facebook.com . To access a specific profile, you can add /[username] to the end of the link.

[59] A **marketplace** is an online space where different sellers can list and sell their products or services to potential buyers.

[60] The official YouTube website can be accessed through the link www.youtube.com .

[61] The official Reddit website can be accessed through the link www.reddit.com .

[62] The official Pinterest website can be accessed through the link www.pinterest.com .

[63] The official Snapchat website can be accessed through the link www.snapchat.com .

[64] You can access the website at this link: https://360suite.google.com/

[65] You can access the website at this link: https://pt.semrush.com/

[66] You can access the website at this link: https://search.google.com/search-console/about

[67] **KPIs** , or Key Performance Indicators, are metrics used to evaluate a company's progress and performance in relation to its strategic objectives. In the context of content marketing, the definition and analysis of KPIs are essential to measure the effectiveness of the strategies adopted.

[68] You can access the website at this link: https://360suite.google.com/

[69] You can access the website at this link: https://search.google.com/search-console/about

[70] You can access the website at this link: https://buzzsumo.com/

[71] You can access the website at this link: https://pt-br.facebook.com/business/insights/tools/audience-insights/

[72] You can access the website at this link: https://analytics.twitter.com/about

[73] You can access the website at this link: https://lookerstudio.google.com/overview

[74] **Benchmarks** refer to standards or reference points that are used to evaluate the performance of a company, project or strategy compared to others in the same industry.

[75] You can access the website at this link: https://trello.com/pt-BR

[76] You can access the website at this link: https://asana.com/pt

[77] You can access the website at this link: https://docs.google.com/

[78] You can access the website at this link: https://www.google.com/intl/pt-BR/sheets/about/

[79] Excel is software that needs to be installed on your device and therefore does not have a direct link for online access. However, you can use Excel Online via the link: www.office.com

[80] You can access the website at this link: https://www.canva.com/pt_br/

www.ingramcontent.com/pod-product-compliance
Lightning Source LLC
Chambersburg PA
CBHW050319230526
45471CB00005B/2263